Collins

KS1 Re... Maths

Maths

Age 5 – 7

Key Stage 1

Practice Workbook

Alan Dobbs and
Janine Hutchinson

Contents

Number – Number and Place Value

Numbers and Counting... 4

Counting Forwards and Backwards 6

Counting in Steps of 2, 3, 5 and 10 8

More and Less 10

Place Value 12

Number – Addition and Subtraction

Solving Number Problems 1 14

Solving Number Problems 2 16

Using Two-Digit Numbers 18

Progress Test 1 20

Number – Multiplication and Division

Multiplication..24

Division 26

Connecting Multiplication and Division 28

Number – Fractions

What is a Fraction? 30

Halves and Quarters 32

Finding Fractions of Larger Groups 34

Progress Test 2 36

Contents

Measurement

Standard Units of Measure 1 40

Standard Units of Measure 2 42

Measuring Time 44

Standard Units of Money 46

Geometry – Properties of Shapes

2-D and 3-D Shapes 48

Different Shapes 50

Progress Test 3 52

Geometry – Position and Direction

Patterns and Sequences 56

Turns 58

Statistics

Pictograms, Charts and Graphs 60

Gathering Information and Using Data 62

Progress Test 4 64

Answers and Progress Test Charts (pull-out) 1–12

Numbers and Counting

Challenge 1

1   Write these in numerals.

a) seventeen   _____   **b)** thirty-one   _____

c) forty-six   _____   **d)** sixty-five   _____

e) ninety-two   _____   **f)** eighty   _____

g) fifteen   _____   **h)** seven   _____

i) twenty-four   _____   **j)** thirteen   _____

10 marks

Marks.........../10

Challenge 2

1   Write these in words.

a) 18 _____   **b)** 12 _____

c) 97 _____   **d)** 42 _____

e) 56 _____   **f)** 23 _____

g) 15 _____   **h)** 70 _____

i) 81 _____   **j)** 79 _____

10 marks

Marks.........../10

Numbers and Counting

Challenge 3

1 Fill in the missing numbers.

   a) 1 2 3 ___ 5 ___ 7 8 ___ 10 11 ___ 13

   b) 65 66 ___ ___ 69 70 ___ 72 73 ___ 75 ___ 77

   c) 20 ___ ___ 17 ___ ___ ___ ___ 12 ___ 10

   d) ___ 58 57 ___ ___ 54 ___ ___ 51 50 ___ 48 ___ 46

4 marks

2 Write the numbers, in order, on the answer line.

   a) 8 4 12 20 13 15

   _____

   b) 27 18 26 22 12 21

   _____

   c) 50 48 15 24 36 19

   _____

   d) 97 82 14 37 65 9

   _____

   e) 79 91 15 13 22 44

   _____

5 marks

Marks.......... /9

Total marks .... /29   How am I doing?

Counting Forwards and Backwards

PS ⟩ Problem-solving questions

Challenge 1

1 Start at 15 and count back the given amounts.

   a) Count back 5 = _____   **b)** Count back 11 = _____

2 marks

2 Start at 22 and count forwards the given amounts.

   a) Count forwards 4 = _____   **b)** Count forwards 3 = _____

2 marks

 3 Six puppies are asleep in a basket. Three of them wake up and go outside to play.

   How many puppies are still asleep in the basket? _____

1 mark

PS ⟩ **4** Ten apples were in the fruit bowl. Jemima took three of them to share with her friends.

   How many apples were left in the bowl? _____

1 mark

Marks.......... /6

Challenge 2

1 Complete the missing numbers in the number square.

0	1	2	3	4	5	6	7	8	
10	11		13	14		16	17	18	19
20	21	22	23		25	26	27	28	29
30	31	32		34	35	36	37	38	39
40	41		43	44	45	46	47	48	49
50	51	52	53	54	55	56		58	59
60	61	62	63	64	65	66	67	68	
70	71	72	73	74	75	76	77	78	79
80		82	83	84	85	86	87	88	89
90	91	92		94	95	96	97	98	99

5 marks

Marks.......... /5

Counting Forwards and Backwards

Challenge 3

PS **1** Sarah had 42 sweets in her bag. She added eight more.

How many sweets did Sarah then have? _____

PS **2** There are 15 fish swimming in the river and five get caught.

How many fish are left in the river? _____

3 Complete the missing numbers on the number caterpillar.

4 Write the next five numbers in these.

a) 15 17 19 21 _____ _____ _____ _____ _____

b) 18 16 14 12 10 _____ _____ _____ _____ _____

c) 12 14 16 18 20 _____ _____ _____ _____ _____

5 a) Put the numbers in order to make a sequence of counting forwards in 10s.

| 31 | 51 | 61 | 21 | 11 | 1 | 41 |

_____

b) Put the numbers in order to make a sequence of counting backwards in 10s.

_____

Marks.......... /9

Total marks .... /20   How am I doing?

Counting in Steps of 2, 3, 5 and 10

PS ⟩ **Problem-solving questions**

Challenge 1

1 Complete the sequence of numbers counting in tens.

   a) 10 20 _____ 40 _____ 60 70 _____ _____ 100

   b) 100 90 80 _____ _____ 50 _____ 30 _____ 10

   2 marks

2 Complete the sequence of numbers counting in twos.

   a) 2 _____ _____ 8 10 _____ 14 _____ 18 _____ 22 24

   b) 24 _____ 20 18 _____ _____ 12 10 _____ 6 _____ 2

   2 marks

3 Complete the sequence of numbers counting in fives.

   a) 5 10 _____ 20 25 _____ 35 _____ 45 50 _____ 60

   b) 95 90 _____ 80 _____ 70 65 _____ 55 _____ 45

   2 marks

4 Complete the sequence of numbers counting in threes.

   a) 3 _____ 9 12 _____ 18 _____ 24 _____ 30

   b) 30 27 _____ 21 18 15 _____ _____ 6 3

   2 marks

5 Complete these number sequences.

   a) 0 _____ 2 _____ 4 _____ 6 _____ 8 _____ 10 _____ 12

   b) 15 _____ 17 _____ 19 _____ 21 _____ 23 _____ 25

   2 marks

Marks......... /10

Challenge 2

1 Write in the missing numbers counting in lots of two.

12			18			24

   2 marks

8

Counting in Steps of 2, 3, 5 and 10

2 Write in the missing numbers counting in lots of three.

3			12			21	

2 marks

3 Look at the sequences of numbers and decide what steps they are counted in.

a) 15 20 25 30 35   Steps of _____.

b) 33 36 39 42 45   Steps of _____.

2 marks

Marks.......... /6

Challenge 3

PS **1** You have four pairs of socks and you get six more pairs.

How many socks do you have? _____

I counted in steps of _____.

2 marks

PS **2** How many toes are there on five feet? _____

I counted in steps of _____.

2 marks

Marks.......... /4

Total marks .... /20   How am I doing?

More and Less

Challenge 1

1 Complete the table below by drawing and writing the correct number of spots. The first one is done for you.

	If there is one spot less, draw and write the correct number of spots.	How many spots? Write the correct number of spots beside each drawing.	If there is one spot more, draw and write the correct number of spots.
a)	●●● ●● 5	●●● ●●● 6	●●●● ●●● 7
b)		●●●●●● ●●●●●●	
c)		●●●● ●●●● ●	
d)		●●●●●● ●●●●● ●	
e)		●●●	

12 marks

Marks.........../12

Challenge 2

1 Write one more than the given numbers.

    a) 7 _____　　　　**b)** 13 _____

    c) 29 _____　　　　**d)** 56 _____

    e) 71 _____　　　　**f)** 49 _____

6 marks

2 Write one less than the given numbers.

    a) 12 _____　　　　**b)** 28 _____

    c) 52 _____　　　　**d)** 90 _____

    e) 67 _____　　　　**f)** 30 _____

6 marks

Marks.........../12

More and Less

Challenge 3

1 Use the symbols <, > and = to compare the numbers.

a) 67 ☐ 49   **b)** 56 ☐ 53

c) 12 ☐ 9   **d)** 99 ☐ 101

e) 100 ☐ 100   **f)** 78 ☐ 78

g) 48 ☐ 32   **h)** 133 ☐ 132

i) 120 ☐ 113   **j)** 111 ☐ 121

10 marks

2 Use the symbols < and > to compare the numbers written in words.

a) eighteen ☐ nine

b) sixty-one ☐ seventy-five

c) twenty-two ☐ ninety-three

d) twelve ☐ forty

e) eighty-four ☐ fifty-six

5 marks

Marks......... /15

Total marks .... /39

How am I doing?

11

Place Value

1 Write down the number that the cubes represent.

a)

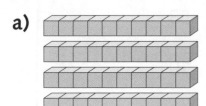 

_____

b)

_____

c)

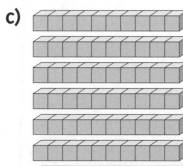

_____

3 marks

2 Write the value of the coins.

a)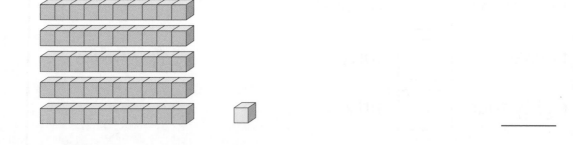

_____

b)

_____

c)

_____

3 marks

Marks.......... /6

Place Value

Challenge 2

1 Write the number that is on each abacus. One has been done.

a) 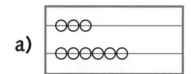 36

b) 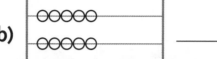 _____

c) 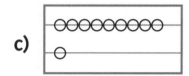 _____

d)  _____

e) 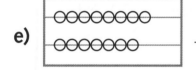 _____

f) 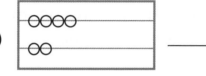 _____

5 marks

Marks.......... /5

Challenge 3

1 Partition these two-digit numbers into tens and ones.

Example: 56 = 50 + 6

a) 42 _____

b) 65 _____

2 marks

2 Write the two-digit number made when the tens and ones are combined.

Example: 40 + 2 = 42

a) 30 + 5 = _____

b) 80 + 1 = _____

2 marks

Marks.......... /4

Total marks .... /15

How am I doing?

Solving Number Problems I

Challenge I

PS 1 How many fish are there altogether? Write the addition sum and answer.

_____ + _____ = _____

2 marks

PS 2 There are eight people on a bus and five more want to get on at the next stop. How many people will be on the bus? Write the addition sum and answer.

_____ + _____ = _____

2 marks

PS 3 Combine the apples to find the total. Write the addition sum and answer.

_____ + _____ = _____

2 marks

PS 4 There were four boys and five girls in a line. How many children were there altogether?

_____ + _____ = _____

2 marks

PS 5 Jack had eight sweets and Nadine had seven sweets. How many sweets did they have altogether?

_____ + _____ = _____

2 marks

Marks......... /10

14

Solving Number Problems 1

Challenge 2

1 Use the pictures to help you take away.

a) 🍓🍓🍓🍓🍓🍓🍓🍓🍓🍓🍓🍓 ___ – 5 = ___

b) 🍓🍓🍓🍓🍓🍓🍓🍓🍓🍓🍓🍓🍓🍓 ___ – 6 = ___

c) 🍓🍓🍓🍓🍓🍓🍓🍓🍓 ___ – 7 = ___

d) 🍓🍓🍓🍓🍓🍓🍓🍓🍓🍓 ___ – 8 = ___

e) 🍓🍓🍓🍓🍓🍓🍓🍓 ___ – 2 = ___

f) 🍓🍓🍓🍓🍓🍓🍓 ___ – 6 = ___

12 marks

Marks.........../12

Challenge 3

1 Use the number line to solve the addition and subtraction sums. Remember to jump forwards for addition and jump backwards for subtraction.

```
+----+----+----+----+----+----+----+----+----+----+----+----+----+----+----+----+----+----+----+----+
0    1    2    3    4    5    6    7    8    9   10   11   12   13   14   15   16   17   18   19   20
```

a) 12 + 7 = _____   b) 14 – 3 = _____

c) 8 + 4 = _____   d) 9 + 11 = _____

e) 7 + 6 = _____   f) 15 – 10 = _____

g) 20 – 8 = _____   h) 17 – 9 = _____

8 marks

Marks.........../8

Total marks ..../30   How am I doing?

Solving Number Problems 2

PS Problem-solving questions

Challenge 1

1 Write the totals of these numbers. Then check your answers by adding in a different order.

a) 3 + 9 + 4 = _____   _____

b) 1 + 7 + 2 = _____   _____

c) 5 + 12 + 4 = _____   _____

d) 9 + 4 + 7 = _____   _____

e) 8 + 10 + 10 = _____   _____

5 marks

Marks.......... /5

Challenge 2

PS **1** Draw pictures on a separate piece of paper to help you solve these subtraction problems.

a) Reanna has 24 packets of crisps. She gives 11 packets to her friends.

How many packets of crisps does Reanna have left? _____

2 marks

b) Mohammed had 30 books. He took six of them back to the library.

How many books does he have now? _____

2 marks

c) Holly has 16 badges. She gives five to her friend Sophie.

How many badges does Holly have now? _____

2 marks

Solving Number Problems 2

d) Dylan has 26 pens. He gives Jack nine of them.

How many pens does Dylan have left? _____

2 marks

e) Giselle has 12 biscuits and she shares six of them with her friends.

How many biscuits does she have left? _____

2 marks

Marks.........../10

Challenge 3

1 Complete the table. The first one has been done for you.

Number problem	+ or −	Number sentence
a) Amelia has 14 books, Sophie has 12. How many books do they have altogether?	+	14 + 12 = 26
b) Jack, Dylan and Luke all have seven cars. How many cars do they have altogether?		
c) There are 18 boys and seven girls in Year 2. How many children are there altogether?		
d) Ellis had 23 crayons, Liz took 11 of them. How many crayons does Ellis have now?		
e) George went to the shop and bought 3 apples, 2 oranges and 4 bananas. How many pieces of fruit did he buy?		

10 marks

Marks.........../10

Total marks ..../25   How am I doing?

Using Two-Digit Numbers

PS Problem-solving questions

Challenge 1

1 Use the numbers 12, 20 and 8 to make the addition and subtraction fact family correct.

a) _____ + 12 = _____

b) _____ + 8 = _____

c) _____ – _____ = 8

d) _____ – _____ = 12

4 marks

2 Fill in the missing number operation symbols (– or +).

a) 5 ☐ 7 = 12

b) 15 ☐ 5 = 10

2 marks

3 Use the numbers 24, 16 and 40 to create the addition and subtraction number sentences.

a) _____ + _____ = _____

b) _____ + _____ = _____

c) _____ – _____ = _____

d) _____ – _____ = _____

4 marks

Marks......... /10

Challenge 2

1 Solve the following addition number sentences. Remember to add the tens and then the units (ones).

a) 71 + 16 = _____

b) 24 + 23 = _____

c) 55 + 33 = _____

d) 87 + 11 = _____

e) 46 + 23 = _____

f) 42 + 12 = _____

6 marks

2 Solve the following subtraction number sentences. Remember to count back the number of tens from the smallest number and then count back in ones.

a) 55 – 21 = _____

b) 89 – 36 = _____

Using Two-Digit Numbers

c) 44 – 11 = _____

d) 73 – 10 = _____

e) 99 – 12 = _____

f) 58 – 28 = _____

6 marks

Marks.........../12

Challenge 3

PS **1** Solve the following number problems. Show the sum you have done to find the answer.

a) Alan has 26 marbles. Liz has 13 less marbles. How many does Liz have?

_____

b) James runs 80 metres. Janine runs 110 metres. How much further does Janine run than James?

_____

c) There are 32 children in Year 4 and 33 in Year 5. How many children are there in Years 4 and 5?

_____

d) A pineapple costs 80p and an apple costs 35p. How much more does the pineapple cost?

_____

8 marks

Marks.........../8

Total marks ..../30   How am I doing?

19

Progress Test 1

1 Complete the addition and subtraction fact family for these numbers.

 16   36   20

a) _____ + _____ = _____   **b)** _____ + _____ = _____

c) _____ – _____ = _____   **d)** _____ – _____ = _____

4 marks

2 Complete the number sequences.

a) 46 _____ 48 _____ 50 _____ 52 _____ 54 _____ 56

b) 21 _____ 41 _____ 61 _____ 81 _____ 101

c) 100 _____ _____ 70 _____ _____ 40 30 20 _____

d) 24 _____ 18 _____ 12 _____ 6 _____

e) 46 _____ 50 _____ 54 56 _____ _____ 62 _____

5 marks

3 Partition the two-digit numbers into tens and ones.

a) 46 = _____ tens _____ units (ones)

b) 55 = _____ tens _____ units (ones)

c) 92 = _____ tens _____ units (ones)

d) 34 = _____ tens _____ units (ones)

e) 28 = _____ tens _____ units (ones)

f) 72 = _____ tens _____ units (ones)

6 marks

PS 4 Solve the following number problems. You need to use the pictures to answer them.

a) How many apples are there altogether?

_____ + _____ = _____

b) A monkey eats two of these bananas. How many are left?

_____ – _____ = _____

c) A monkey eats four of these bananas. How many are left?

_____ – _____ = _____

3 marks

PS Problem-solving questions

5 The numbers on the paper chains have a total of 10. Write the missing numbers.

a)  5 _____

b)  6 _____

c)  7 _____

d)  8 _____

e)  9 _____

f)  10 _____

g) 1 _____

h) 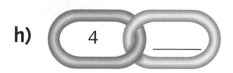 4 _____

4 marks

6 Write the digits to match the words.

a) forty-six _____

b) twenty-five _____

c) nineteen _____

d) eighty-one _____

e) thirty-four _____

f) fifty-seven _____

g) sixty-three _____

h) ninety-one _____

4 marks

7 Solve the following number problems.

a) $65 + 33 =$ _____

b) $78 + 15 =$ _____

c) $42 + 23 =$ _____

d) $31 + 22 =$ _____

2 marks

8 Put the numbers in order from smallest to largest.

 55 12 6 84 36 21

1 mark

9 Write the numbers that are 10 less than each of these.

| 136 | 84 | 95 | 10 | 41 |

____   ____   ____   ____   ____

5 marks

10 Subtract 9 from 27. _____

1 mark

11 Use <, > or = to make these number pairs correct.

a) 12 ⬚ 12   **b)** 59 ⬚ 41   **c)** 78 ⬚ 99

d) 44 ⬚ 62   **e)** 32 ⬚ 29   **f)** 63 ⬚ 63

3 marks

12 Write one more than the given numbers.

a) 12 _____   **b)** 8 _____   **c)** 23 _____

d) 34 _____   **e)** 82 _____   **f)** 13 _____

3 marks

13 Write one less than the given numbers.

a) 18 _____   **b)** 89 _____   **c)** 32 _____

d) 10 _____   **e)** 13 _____   **f)** 55 _____

3 marks

PS **14** Joshua swims 50 metres and Daisy swims 25 metres.

How many more metres did Joshua swim? _____

1 mark

PS **15** Yusuf had 25 sweets. He gave five sweets to Henry, five sweets to Jasmine and five sweets to Ella.

How many sweets did he have left for himself?

_____

1 mark

Marks........ /46

23

Multiplication

Challenge 1

1 Shade the numbers which are products when you multiply by 5.

1	2	3	4	5	6	7	8	9	10
11	12	13	14	15	16	17	18	19	20
21	22	23	24	25	26	27	28	29	30
31	32	33	34	35	36	37	38	39	40
41	42	43	44	45	46	47	48	49	50

5 marks

2 Multiply the number of grapes in each bunch by 2.

a) _____

b) _____

c) _____

d) _____

e) _____

5 marks

Marks......... /10

Challenge 2

1 How much money is there altogether?

___ + ___ + ___ + ___ + ___ + ___ + ___ + ___ + ___ = ___p

2 marks

Multiplication

2 How many fish are there altogether?

_____ + _____ + _____ + _____ = _____

2 marks

3 How many socks can you see altogether?

____ + ____ + ____ + ____ + ____ + ____ + ____ + ____ = ____

2 marks

Marks.......... /6

Challenge 3

PS **1** Sienna loved to read. She read five pages every night for 10 nights.

How many pages did she read altogether?

_____

1 mark

PS **2** Milo saved £1 every week for six weeks.

How much money did he save?

_____

1 mark

PS **3** Amara eats two bananas every day for seven days.

How many bananas does she eat?

_____

1 mark

Marks.......... /3

Total marks .... /19   How am I doing?

Division

Challenge 1

⟩PS⟩ **1** You want to share 10 sweets equally between two people.

    a) How many sweets will each person get?_____

    b) Write it as a division sum. _____ ÷ _____ = _____

 2 marks

⟩PS⟩ **2** There are five people and they are all hungry. Share 20 sandwiches equally, so every person gets the same amount.

    a) Each person will get _____ sandwiches.

    b) Write it as a division sum. _____ ÷ _____ = _____

 2 marks

⟩PS⟩ **3** Write a division sum for each statement.

    a) 30 marbles are divided between 10 people. How many marbles does each person get?

    _____ ÷ _____ = _____

    b) 24 marbles are divided between two people. How many marbles does each person get?

    _____ ÷ _____ = _____

 2 marks

Marks.......... /6

Challenge 2

⟩PS⟩ **1** Jack has 20p.

    a) If he has only 5p coins, how many coins does he have?_____

    b) If he has only 10p coins, how many coins does he have?_____

 2 marks

Division

PS **2** Hafsah has 10p.

a) If she has only 2p coins, how many coins does she have?_____

b) If she has only 1p coins, how many coins does she have?_____

2 marks

3 Solve these division problems.

a) $12 \div 6 =$ _____

b) $50 \div 5 =$ _____

2 marks

PS **4** Laura completes two lengths of a swimming pool and swims 50 metres. How many metres is one length of the pool?

_____

1 mark

Marks........../7

Challenge 3

PS **1** Show your working out. Write the division sum.

a) A shop has 28 bouncy balls and they need to be put in boxes of 7. How many boxes are needed?

_____ $\div$ _____ = _____

2 marks

b) Flowers are sold in bunches of 5. There are 20 flowers. How many bunches can be made?

_____ $\div$ _____ = _____

2 marks

c) Rubbers cost 3p each. Mac has 21p. How many rubbers can he buy?

_____ $\div$ _____ = _____

2 marks

Marks........../6

Total marks .... /19   How am I doing?

Connecting Multiplication and Division

 PS Problem-solving questions

Challenge 1

1 Solve these number problems.

a) $2 \times 5 =$ _____

b) $3 \times 3 =$ _____

c) $12 \div 2 =$ _____

d) $21 \div 3 =$ _____

4 marks

2 Draw the correct number of spots in the circles by reading the description below each one.

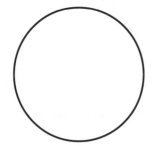 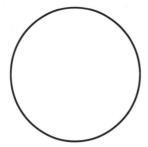 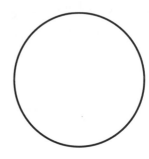

a) Double 9

b) Double 10

c) Double 7

3 marks

Marks.......... /7

Challenge 2

1 Use the numbers 10, 50 and 5 to make the multiplication and division number sentences correct.

a) _____ × 10 = _____

b) _____ ÷ _____ = 5

2 marks

2 Use the numbers 3, 33 and 11 to make the multiplication and division number sentences correct.

a) 11 × _____ = _____

b) _____ ÷ _____ = 3

2 marks

3 Fill in the missing number operation symbol (× or ÷).

a) 5 ☐ 2 = 10

b) 15 ☐ 3 = 5

2 marks

Connecting Multiplication and Division

4 Halve these numbers by sharing them equally between two.

a) Half of 10 = _____   b) Half of 8 = _____

c) Half of 6 = _____   d) Half of 4 = _____

2 marks

Marks.......... /8

Challenge 3

1 Use the numbers 24, 6 and 4 to create the multiplication and division number sentences.

a) _____ × _____ = _____   b) _____ ÷ _____ = _____

2 marks

2 Use the numbers 30, 5 and 6 to create the multiplication and division number sentences.

a) _____ × _____ = _____   b) _____ ÷ _____ = _____

2 marks

PS **3** Adam is four years old, Joseph is double his age and Geoff is double Joseph's age.

How old is Geoff? _____

1 mark

4 In January, it normally snows for nine days. Last year, it snowed for double that time.

How many days did it snow for last year? _____

1 mark

5 Granny baked 12 apple pies and Mum baked half as many.

How many apple pies did Mum make? _____

1 mark

Marks.......... /7

Total marks .... /22   How am I doing?

What is a Fraction?

Challenge 1

1   These four pizzas are being prepared. Draw lines to match each fraction with a pizza to show how much of each pizza has been prepared.

A

$\frac{1}{2}$

B

$\frac{1}{4}$

C

1 whole

D

$\frac{3}{4}$

4 marks

2   What fraction of these pizzas in question 1 has **not** yet been prepared?

a) A = ☐   b) B = ☐   c) C = ☐

3 marks

 Marks.......... /7

Challenge 2

1   How many quarters do these fractions have?

a) $\frac{1}{2}$ _____   b) $\frac{1}{4}$ _____

c) $\frac{3}{4}$ _____   d) 1 whole _____

4 marks

What is a Fraction?

2 Colour three-quarters of each shape.

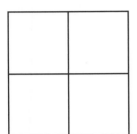 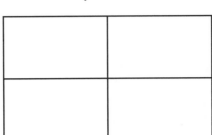

2 marks

Marks.......... /6

Challenge 3

1 Use the correct symbol (<, > or =) to describe these fractions.

a) $\frac{1}{4}$ ☐ $\frac{1}{2}$ **b)** $\frac{3}{4}$ ☐ $\frac{1}{2}$

c) $\frac{2}{4}$ ☐ $\frac{1}{2}$ **d)** $\frac{2}{2}$ ☐ $\frac{4}{4}$

4 marks

2 Look at the pictures.

a) Colour a quarter of circle A.

b) Colour three-quarters of circle B.

c) Colour half of circle C.

Circle A   Circle B   Circle C

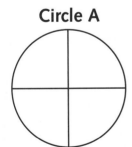 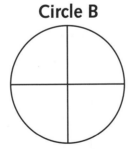 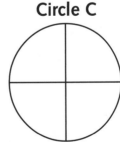

3 marks

3 Put the correct fraction in the boxes.

a) 5 is of 10   **b)** 3 is ☐ of 12

2 marks

Marks.......... /9

Total marks .... /22   How am I doing?

Halves and Quarters

Challenge 1

1 Colour $\frac{1}{2}$ of block A.

Colour $\frac{3}{4}$ of block B.

Colour $\frac{1}{2}$ of block C.

Colour $\frac{1}{4}$ of block D.

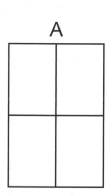 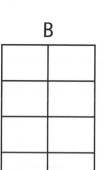 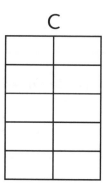 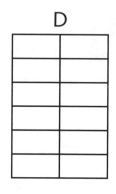

A   B   C   D

4 marks

PS **2** Which block in question 1 shows the largest fraction? _____

1 mark

3 Order these from least to most: $\frac{3}{4}$ $\frac{1}{4}$ 0 $\frac{1}{2}$ 1

1 mark

Marks.......... /6

Challenge 2

PS ⟩ **1 a)** What fraction of each circle is missing?

A   B   C   D

A = ☐   B = ☐   C = ☐   D = ☐

4 marks

Halves and Quarters

b) What fraction of each circle remains?

A = ☐ B = ☐ C = ☐ D = ☐

4 marks

c) Which circle has the most missing? _____

1 mark

d) Which circle has the least missing? _____

1 mark

Marks......... /10

Challenge 3

PS **1** Here are three bags of sweets.

A B C

a) Which bag contains half the sweets of bag C? _____

b) How many sweets would be half of bag A? _____

c) How many sweets would be $\frac{3}{4}$ of bag C? _____

d) How many sweets would be $\frac{1}{2}$ of bag B? _____

e) What fraction is three sweets of bag C? ☐

5 marks

2 Find half of these numbers.

a) Half of 20 is _____

b) Half of 16 is _____

2 marks

Marks......... /7

Total marks .... /23   How am I doing?

Finding Fractions of Larger Groups

Challenge 1

PS **1** The number is 20.

a) What is $\frac{1}{2}$ of the number? _____

b) What would $\frac{1}{4}$ of the number be? _____

c) What would $\frac{3}{4}$ of the number be? _____

d) What would $\frac{2}{4}$ of the number be? _____

e) How much is the whole number? _____

5 marks

Marks.......... /5

Challenge 2

PS **1** Look at the coins.

a) How much is $\frac{1}{2}$ of the amount? _____ p

b) How much is $\frac{1}{4}$ of the amount? _____ p

c) What fraction of the whole amount is 9p? ⬚

d) 3p is ⬚ of the whole amount.

e) $\frac{2}{4}$ of the whole amount would be _____ p.

5 marks

2 How much is half of these amounts?

a) 20p _____ p   b) 30p _____ p

c) 50p _____ p   d) 10p _____ p

e) £1 _____ p   f) 80p _____ p

6 marks

Marks.......... /11

Answers

Pages 4–5
Challenge 1
1 a) 17
   b) 31
   c) 46
   d) 65
   e) 92
   f) 80
   g) 15
   h) 7
   i) 24
   j) 13

Challenge 2
1 a) eighteen
   b) twelve
   c) ninety-seven
   d) forty-two
   e) fifty-six
   f) twenty-three
   g) fifteen
   h) seventy
   i) eighty-one
   j) seventy-nine

Challenge 3
1 a) 1, 2, 3, **4**, 5, **6**, 7, 8, **9**, 10, 11, **12**, 13
   b) 65, 66, **67**, **68**, 69, 70, **71**, 72, 73, **74**, 75, **76**, 77
   c) 20, **19**, **18**, 17, **16**, **15**, **14**, **13**, 12, **11**, 10
   d) **59**, 58, 57, **56**, **55**, 54, **53**, **52**, 51, 50, **49**, 48, **47**, 46
2 a) 4, 8, 12, 13, 15, 20
   b) 12, 18, 21, 22, 26, 27
   c) 15, 19, 24, 36, 48, 50
   d) 9, 14, 37, 65, 82, 97
   e) 13, 15, 22, 44, 79, 91

Pages 6–7
Challenge 1
1 a) 10
   b) 4
2 a) 26
   b) 25
3 3
4 7

Challenge 2
1 9, 12, 15, 24, 33, 42, 57, 69, 81, 93

Challenge 3
1 50
2 10
3 10, **11**, 12, **13**, 14, **15**, 16, **17**, 18, **19**, 20, **21**

4 a) 23, 25, 27, 29, 31
   b) 8, 6, 4, 2, 0
   c) 22, 24, 26, 28, 30
5 a) 1, 11, 21, 31, 41, 51, 61
   b) 61, 51, 41, 31, 21, 11, 1

Pages 8–9
Challenge 1
1 a) 10, 20, **30**, 40, **50**, 60, 70, **80**, **90**, 100
   b) 100, 90, 80, **70**, **60**, 50, **40**, 30, **20**, 10
2 a) 2, **4**, **6**, 8, 10, **12**, 14, **16**, 18, **20**, 22, 24
   b) 24, **22**, 20, 18, **16**, **14**, 12, 10, **8**, 6, **4**, 2
3 a) 5, 10, **15**, 20, 25, **30**, 35, **40**, 45, 50, **55**, 60
   b) 95, 90, **85**, 80, **75**, 70, 65, **60**, 55, **50**, 45
4 a) 3, **6**, 9, 12, **15**, 18, **21**, 24, **27**, 30
   b) 30, 27, **24**, 21 18, 15, **12**, **9**, 6, 3
5 a) 0, **1**, 2, **3**, 4, **5**, 6, **7**, 8, **9**, 10, **11**, 12
   b) 15, **16**, 17, **18**, 19, **20**, 21, **22**, 23, **24**, 25

Challenge 2
1 12, **14**, **16**, 18, **20**, **22**, 24
2 3, **6**, **9**, 12, **15**, **18**, 21, **24**
3 a) Steps of 5.
   b) Steps of 3.

Challenge 3
1 20. I counted in steps of 2.
2 25. I counted in steps of 5.

Pages 10–11
Challenge 1
1 b) ⬛⬛⬛⬛⬛⬛◦ 11, 12, ⬛⬛⬛⬛⬛⬛◦ 13
   c) ⬛⬛⬛⬛ 8, 9, ⬛⬛⬛⬛⬛ 10
   d) ⬛⬛⬛⬛⬛⬛ 12, 13, ⬛⬛⬛⬛⬛⬛⬛ 14
   e) •• 2, 3, ⬛⬛ 4

Challenge 2
1 a) 8
   b) 14
   c) 30
   d) 57
   e) 72
   f) 50

2 a) 11
   b) 27
   c) 51
   d) 89
   e) 66
   f) 29

Challenge 3
1 a) 67 > 49
   b) 56 > 53
   c) 12 > 9
   d) 99 < 101

1

Answers

e) 100 = 100
f) 78 = 78
g) 48 > 32
h) 133 > 132
i) 120 > 113
j) 111 < 121

2 a) eighteen > nine
   b) sixty-one < seventy-five
   c) twenty-two < ninety-three
   d) twelve < forty
   e) eighty-four > fifty-six

Pages 12–13
Challenge 1
1 a) 45 b) 27 c) 71
2 a) 50p b) 32p c) 45p

Challenge 2
1 a) 36
   b) 55
   c) 91
   d) 13
   e) 87
   f) 42

Challenge 3
1 a) 40 + 2 b) 60 + 5
2 a) 35 b) 81

Pages 14–15
Challenge 1
1 6 + 3 = 9
2 8 + 5 = 13
3 12 + 5 = 17
4 4 + 5 = 9
5 8 + 7 = 15

Challenge 2
1 a) 12 – 5 = 7
   b) 14 – 6 = 8
   c) 9 – 7 = 2
   d) 10 – 8 = 2
   e) 8 – 2 = 6
   f) 7 – 6 = 1

Challenge 3
1 a) 19
   b) 11
   c) 12
   d) 20
   e) 13
   f) 5
   g) 12
   h) 8

Pages 16–17
Challenge 1
1 a) 16 (9 + 4 + 3 = 16)
   b) 10 (2 + 1 + 7 = 10)
   c) 21 (12 + 4 + 5 = 21)
   d) 20 (4 + 7 + 9 = 20)
   e) 28 (10 + 8 + 10 = 28)

Challenge 2
1 a) 13
   b) 24
   c) 11
   d) 17
   e) 6

Challenge 3
1 a) (+) 14 + 12 = 26
   b) (+) 7 + 7 + 7 = 21
   c) (+) 18 + 7 = 25
   d) (–) 23 – 11 = 12
   e) (+) 3 + 2 + 4 = 9

Pages 18–19
Challenge 1
1 a) 8 + 12 = 20
   b) 12 + 8 = 20
   c) 20 – 12 = 8
   d) 20 – 8 = 12
2 a) + b) –
3 a) – b) 24 + 16 = 40   16 + 24 = 40
   c) – d) 40 – 16 = 24   40 – 24 = 16

Challenge 2
1 a) 87
   b) 47
   c) 88
   d) 98
   e) 69
   f) 54
2 a) 34
   b) 53
   c) 33
   d) 63
   e) 87
   f) 30

Challenge 3
1 a) 26 – 13 = 13 b) 110 – 80 = 30m
   c) 32 + 33 = 65 d) 80 – 35 = 45p

Pages 20–23
Progress Test 1
1 a) – b) 16 + 20 = 36   20 + 16 = 36
   c) – d) 36 – 20 = 16   36 – 16 = 20
2 a) 46, **47**, 48, **49**, 50, **51**, 52, **53**,
      54, **55**, 56

b) 21, **31**, 41, **51**, 61, **71**, 81, **91**, 101

c) 100, **90**, **80**, 70, **60**, **50**, 40, 30, 20, **10**

d) 24, **21**, 18, **15**, 12, **9**, 6, **3**

e) 46, **48**, 50, **52**, 54, 56, **58**, **60**, 62, **64**

3 a) 46 = 4 tens 6 units (ones)

   b) 55 = 5 tens 5 units (ones)

   c) 92 = 9 tens 2 units (ones)

   d) 34 = 3 tens 4 units (ones)

   e) 28 = 2 tens 8 units (ones)

   f) 72 = 7 tens 2 units (ones)

4 a) 5 + 10 = 15

   b) 8 − 2 = 6

   c) 5 − 4 = 1

5 a) 5 b) 4 c) 3 d) 2 e) 1 f) 0

   g) 9 h) 6

6 a) 46   b) 25

   c) 19   d) 81

   e) 34   f) 57

   g) 63   h) 91

7 a) 98

   b) 93

   c) 65

   d) 53

8   6, 12, 21, 36, 55, 84

9   126, 74, 85, 0, 31

10 18

11 a) 12 = 12

    b) 59 > 41

    c) 78 < 99

    d) 44 < 62

    e) 32 > 29

    f) 63 = 63

12 a) 13

    b) 9

    c) 24

    d) 35

    e) 83

    f) 14

13 a) 17

    b) 88

    c) 31

    d) 9

    e) 12

    f) 54

14 25 m

15 10

Pages 24–25
Challenge 1

1

1	2	3	4	5	6	7	8	9	10
11	12	13	14	15	16	17	18	19	20
21	22	23	24	25	26	27	28	29	30
31	32	33	34	35	36	37	38	39	40
41	42	43	44	45	46	47	48	49	50

2 a) 6 b) 20 c) 12 d) 2 e) 18

Challenge 2

1   10 + 10 + 10 + 10 + 10 + 10 + 10 + 10 + 10 = 90p

2   3 + 3 + 3 + 3 = 12

3   2 + 2 + 2 + 2 + 2 + 2 + 2 + 2 = 16

Challenge 3

1   50

2   £6

3   14

Pages 26–27
Challenge 1

1 a) 5

   b) 10 ÷ 2 = 5

2 a) 4

   b) 20 ÷ 5 = 4

3 a) 30 ÷ 10 = 3

   b) 24 ÷ 2 = 12

Challenge 2

1 a) 4

   b) 2

2 a) 5

   b) 10

3 a) 2

   b) 10

4   25

Challenge 3

1 a) 28 ÷ 7 = 4

   b) 20 ÷ 5 = 4

   c) 21 ÷ 3 = 7

Pages 28–29
Challenge 1

1 a) 10   b) 9

   c) 6   d) 7

Answers

2

a)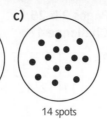

18 spots

b)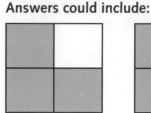

20 spots

c)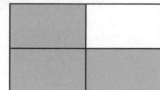

14 spots

Challenge 2

1 a) $5 \times 10 = 50$
   b) $50 \div 10 = 5$
2 a) $11 \times 3 = 33$
   b) $33 \div 11 = 3$
3 a) $\times$
   b) $\div$
4 a) 5
   b) 4
   c) 3
   d) 2

Challenge 3

1 Answers could include:
   a) $6 \times 4 = 24$
       $4 \times 6 = 24$
   b) $24 \div 4 = 6$
       $24 \div 6 = 4$
2 Answers could include:
   a) $5 \times 6 = 30$
       $6 \times 5 = 30$
   b) $30 \div 6 = 5$
       $30 \div 5 = 6$
3 16
4 18
5 6

Pages 30–31
Challenge 1

1 A $\longrightarrow$ $\frac{1}{4}$

   B $\longrightarrow$ $\frac{1}{2}$

   C $\longrightarrow$ $\frac{3}{4}$

   D $\longrightarrow$ 1 whole

2 a) $\frac{3}{4}$

   b) $\frac{1}{2}$

   c) $\frac{1}{4}$

Challenge 2

1 a) 2
   b) 1
   c) 3
   d) 4

2 Answers could include:

Challenge 3

1 a) $\frac{1}{4} < \frac{1}{2}$

   b) $\frac{3}{4} > \frac{1}{2}$

   c) $\frac{2}{4} = \frac{1}{2}$

   d) $\frac{2}{2} = \frac{4}{4}$

2 Answers could include:
   a)

   b)

   c)

3 a) $\frac{1}{2}$

   b) $\frac{1}{4}$

Pages 32–33
Challenge 1

1 Block A = any 2 segments. Block B = any 6 segments. Block C = any 5 segments. Block D = any 3 segments.
2 Block B
3 0, $\frac{1}{4}$, $\frac{1}{2}$, $\frac{3}{4}$, 1

Challenge 2

1 a) A = $\frac{1}{4}$; B = $\frac{3}{4}$; C = $\frac{1}{2}$; D = 0
   b) A = $\frac{3}{4}$; B = $\frac{1}{4}$; C = $\frac{1}{2}$; D = 1
   c) B
   d) D

Challenge 3

1 a) A
   b) 3
   c) 9
   d) 5
   e) $\frac{1}{4}$

2 a) 10
   b) 8

Pages 34–35
Challenge 1
1 a) 10
   b) 5
   c) 15
   d) 10
   e) 20

Challenge 2
1 a) 6p
   b) 3p
   c) $\frac{3}{4}$
   d) $\frac{1}{4}$
   e) 6p
2 a) 10p
   b) 15p
   c) 25p
   d) 5p
   e) 50p
   f) 40p

Challenge 3
1 Any four sections shaded differently on each square.

Pages 36–39
Progress Test 2
1 a) Any two slices coloured.
   b) Any six slices coloured.
   c) Any five slices coloured.
   d) Any three slices coloured.
   e) Pizza B

2 0 $\frac{1}{4}$ $\frac{1}{2}$ $\frac{3}{4}$ 1

3 a) 70
   b) 40
   c) 18
   d) 18
4 a) 50p   10 × 5 = 50 or
     5 + 5 + 5 + 5 + 5 + 5 + 5 + 5 + 5 + 5 = 50p
   b) 18p   9 × 2 = 18 or
     2 + 2 + 2 + 2 + 2 + 2 + 2 + 2 + 2 = 18p
5 a) 55 = 5 tens 5 units (ones)
   b) 74 = 7 tens 4 units (ones)
   c) 92 = 9 tens 2 units (ones)
   d) 18 = 1 ten 8 units (ones)
6 a) $\frac{1}{2} < \frac{3}{4}$
   b) $\frac{1}{1} > \frac{1}{4}$
   c) $\frac{2}{4} = \frac{1}{2}$
   d) $\frac{3}{4} > \frac{1}{4}$
7 a) 8
   b) 10
   c) 10
   d) 10
8 26 − 11 = 15
9 27 + 13 = 40
10 3
11 65, **66**, 67, **68**, **69**, 70, 71
12 a) 16   b) 29
13 a) 5, 8, **11**, **14**, 17, **20**, 23
    b) 60, **55**, 50, 45, **40**, 35, 30, **25**
14 a) 40   b) 10
15 3 + 5 + 7 = 15
16 a) >   b) =   c) <
17 a) 37
    b) 46
    c) 41
    d) 35
18 a) 10 + 1
    b) 90 + 8
19 a) 14
    b) 7
20 Jack: 100
    Nicholas: 1

Pages 40–41
Challenge 1
1 a) D
   b) C
   c) shorter
2 spoon = about 10 cm; van = about 6 m

Challenge 2
1 a) 250 g
   b) 500 g
   c) 150 g
   d) sultanas
   e) 900 g

Challenge 3
1 chocolate bar = about 100 g; leaf = less than 2 g; bike = more than 10 kg; keyboard = about 3 kg

Pages 42–43
Challenge 1
1 a) 3 l
   b) 5 l
   c) jug C
   d) 10 l

Answers

Challenge 2
1 a) 100 ml
  b) 2 scoops
  c) 300 ml
  d) 600 ml
  e) 400 ml

Challenge 3
1 300 ml
2 10
3 450 ml
4 5

Pages 44–45
Challenge 1
1 clock A = 2 o'clock; clock B = half past 2;
  clock C = 3 o'clock; clock D = half past 3.
2 2 o'clock
3 30 minutes

Challenge 2
1 a) B   C   D

  b) 1 hour 30 minutes or $1\frac{1}{2}$ hours

Challenge 3
1 A   B
   3 4:30   4 5:00

2 2 hours 30 minutes
3 B   C   D

4 a) 8:15 (or 20:15)
  b) 5:30 (or 17:30)

Pages 46–47
Challenge 1
1 a) 65p
  b) insect toy
  c) Any combination of available coins, e.g. 20p,
     2p and 1p or 10p, 10p, 2p and 1p
  d) 20p, 10p, 10p, 5p, 5p

Challenge 2
1 a) bunny
  b) 30p
  c) 40p
  d) bunny – insect toy – whistle – mask – car
2 £1.43 or 143p

Challenge 3
1 a) A = 29p; B = 65p; C = 90p
  b) Any combination of available coins, e.g.
     1 × 50p or 20p, 20p and 10p

Pages 48–49
Challenge 1
1 hexagon triangle pentagon circle

2 a) square   b) circle
  c) rectangle   d) hexagon
  e) triangle

Challenge 2
1 C
2
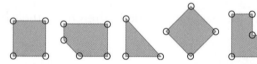

Challenge 3
1 a) Pentagon: five straight sides; five corners
  b) Triangle: three straight sides; three corners
2 A: 6 faces / 8 vertices; B: 3 faces / 0 vertices

Pages 50–51
Challenge 1
1

Shape	Has 6 faces	Has triangular faces
Cuboid	✓	✗
Pyramid	✗	✓

2 sphere cuboid pyramid cone   cube   cylinder

Challenge 2
1 a) circle   b) cylinder   c) cube
2 a)   b) 12

Challenge 3

1

2 **Answers could include:**

Pages 52–55
Progress Test 3

1 a) 63
 b) 51
 c) 48
 d) 25
 e) 19
 f) 5
 g) 33
 h) 76
 i) 87
 j) 90

2 Clock A = 1 o'clock; Clock B = half past 7;
 Clock C = 5 o'clock; Clock D = half past 4

3 **Answers could include:**

4 22 + 12 = 34; 12 + 22 = 34;
 34 − 22 = 12; 34 − 12 = 22

5 a) 69p
 b) Any combination of available coins, e.g.
 20p + 5p or 10p + 5p + 5p + 2p + 2p + 1p
 c) 44p

6 a) **10**, 20, **30**, **40**, 50, **60**, 70, **80**, **90**, 100
 b) 100, **90**, 80, **70**, 60, **50**, 40, 30, **20**, **10**

7 a) $\frac{1}{2}$ b) $\frac{1}{4}$ c) $\frac{1}{2}$ d) $\frac{3}{4}$

8 a) 8 tens 3 units (ones)
 b) 2 tens 9 units (ones)
 c) 1 ten 6 units (ones)

9 A: 4 sides / 4 corners; B: 6 faces / 8 corners

10 a) 10 b) 50 c) 12 d) 5 e) 4 f) 2

11 a) Quarter to ten
 b) Half past five
 c) Quarter past six
 d) Two o'clock

12 16 − 6 = 10

13 **Answers could include:**

14 a) 9 + 3 + 7 = 19
 b) 37 − 12 = 25

15 a) melon = about 1 kg / strawberry = less
 than 20 g / sack of potatoes = more than
 5 kg / banana = about 100 g
 b) sack of potatoes

Pages 56–57
Challenge 1

1

2 | 5 | 5 | 6 | 6 | 7 | 7 |

Challenge 2

1 a) 1
 b) 5
 c) 3
 d) 0

2 a) and b)

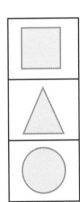

Challenge 3

1

2

	1	
7	3	5
	6	

Answers

Pages 58–59
Challenge 1
1 a) 2
   b) 3
   c) 2
   d) 3

Challenge 2
1 a) 4
   b) 1
   c) 4
   d) 0

Challenge 3
1 a) horse shoe
   b) jewel
   c) coin

Pages 60–61
Challenge 1
1 a) 2
   b) 3
   c) 3
   d) elephant

Challenge 2
1 a) apples
   b) 3
   c) 17

Challenge 3
1 a) 3
   b) 2
   c) 7
   d) car

Pages 62–63
Challenge 1
1 a) 8
   b) 12
   c) 6
   d) 3
   e) 4

Challenge 2

1 a) b)

Sandwich	Tally	Total
Ham	卌 |	6
Cheese	卌 ||	7
Egg	||||	4
Tuna	卌	5
Salad	卌 |	6

Challenge 3
1 a)

Food	Tally	Total
Crisps	卌 卌	10
Jelly	卌 |	6
Buns	卌 ||||	9
Samosas	卌 卌 |	11
Ice-cream	卌 卌	10

b)

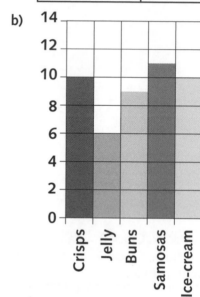

Pages 64–68
Progress Test 4
1 a) C
   b) B
   c) longer
   d) B D A C
2 a) 75 > 59
   b) 14 < 19
   c) 98 = 98
   d) 100 > 99
3 a) 5
   b) 10
   c) 8
   d) 20
4
5 6 6 5 5 4 4
6 3 3 3 2 2 1
7 a) 6
   b) 3
   c) 4
8 a) 12 ÷ 2 = 6
   b) 12 ÷ 4 = 3
   c) 12 ÷ 3 = 4

9

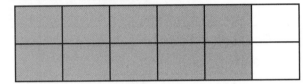

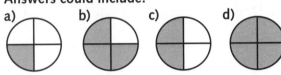

10 **Answers could include:**
a) b) c) d)

11 **30**, 27, **24**, **21**, 18, 15, **12**
12 20; I counted in steps of 2
13 10

14

Shape	Has 8 corners	Has circular faces
Cuboid	✓	✗
Cylinder	✗	✓

15 a) 66, 77, 88
b) colour the odd numbers red – 33, 55, 77; colour the even numbers blue – 44, 66, 88

16

Class	Tally	Total
1	ⅬⅡ ⅬⅡ ‖	12
2	ⅬⅡ ⅬⅡ ‖‖	14
3	ⅬⅡ ‖‖	8
4	ⅬⅡ ⅬⅡ	10

17 a) mouse
b) fox
c) cow
18 a) 3
b) 4
c) 4
d) 2

Progress Test Charts

Progress Test 1

Q	Topic	✓ or X	See page
1	Using Two-Digit Numbers		18
2	Counting Forwards and Backwards		6
3	Place Value		12
4	Solving Number Problems		14, 16
5	Solving Number Problems		14, 16
6	Numbers and Counting		4
7	Using Two-Digit Numbers		18
8	More and Less		10
9	Counting in Steps of 2, 3, 5 and 10		8
10	Solving Number Problems		14, 16
11	More and Less		10
12	More and Less		10
13	More and Less		10
14	Solving Number Problems		14, 16
15	Solving Number Problems		14, 16

Progress Test 2

Q	Topic	✓ or X	See page
1	Halves and Quarters		32
2	What is a Fraction?		30
3	Multiplication		24
4	Counting in Steps of 2, 3, 5 and 10		8
5	Place Value		12
6	More and Less, What is a Fraction?		10, 30
7	Division		26
8	Solving Number Problems		14, 16
9	Solving Number Problems		14, 16
10	Finding Fractions of Larger Groups		34
11	Numbers and Counting		4
12	Counting Forwards and Backwards		6
13	Counting in Steps of 2, 3, 5 and 10		8
14	Connecting Multiplication and Division		28
15	Solving Number Problems		14, 16
16	More and Less		10
17	Solving Number Problems		14, 16
18	Place Value		12
19	Finding Fractions of Larger Groups		34
20	Connecting Multiplication and Division		28

Progress Test 3

Q	Topic	✓ or X	See page
1	Numbers and Counting		4
2	Measuring Time		44
3	Halves and Quarters		32
4	Using Two-Digit Numbers		18
5	Standard Units of Money		46
6	Counting in Steps of 2, 3, 5 and 10		8
7	What is a Fraction?		30
8	Place Value		12
9	2-D and 3-D Shapes		48
10	Multiplication, Division		24, 26
11	Measuring Time		44
12	Solving Number Problems		14, 16
13	Different Shapes		50
14	Solving Number Problems		14, 16
15	Standard Units of Measure		40, 42

Progress Test 4

Q	Topic	✓ or X	See page
1	Standard Units of Measure		40, 42
2	More and Less		10
3	Finding Fractions of Larger Groups		34
4	Patterns and Sequences		56
5	Patterns and Sequences		56
6	Patterns and Sequences		56
7	Division		26
8	Division		26
9	Multiplication		24
10	What is a Fraction?, Halves and Quarters		30, 32
11	Counting in Steps of 2, 3, 5 and 10		8
12	Counting in Steps of 2, 3, 5 and 10		8
13	Multiplication		24
14	2-D and 3-D Shapes, Different Shapes		48, 50
15	Patterns and Sequences		56
16	Gathering Information and Using Data		62
17	Turns		58
18	Pictograms, Charts and Graphs		60

What am I doing well in? _____

_____

What do I need to improve? _____

_____

Finding Fractions of Larger Groups

1 Shade half of each square and try to make each pattern different.

A 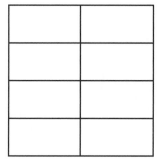   B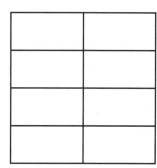

C 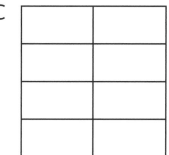   D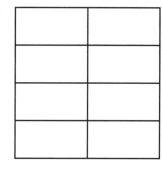

E 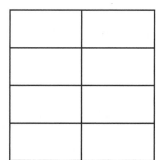   F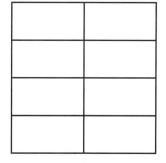

G 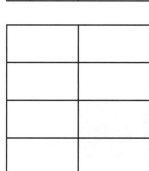   H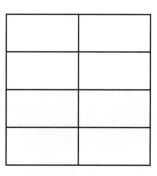

8 marks

Marks.......... /8

Total marks .... /24   How am I doing?

Progress Test 2

PS **1** **a)** Colour $\frac{1}{2}$ of pizza A.

     b) Colour $\frac{3}{4}$ of pizza B.

     c) Colour $\frac{1}{2}$ of pizza C.

     d) Colour $\frac{1}{4}$ of pizza D.

     e) Which pizza shows the largest fraction? _____

A 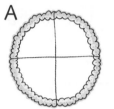 B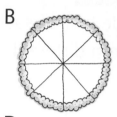

C   D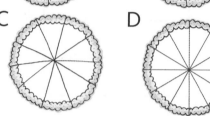

5 marks

2 Order these from least to most: $\frac{1}{2}$ $\frac{1}{4}$ 1 $\frac{3}{4}$ 0

_____

1 mark

3 Solve these multiplication number problems.

     a) $7 \times 10 =$ _____   **b)** $8 \times 5 =$ _____

     c) $6 \times 3 =$ _____   **d)** $9 \times 2 =$ _____

4 marks

4 How much money is there? Write down the number sentences you made.

   a)

_____

   b)

_____

2 marks

36

5 Partition the two-digit numbers into tens and units (ones).

    a) 55 = _____ tens _____ units (ones)

    b) 74 = _____ tens _____ units (ones)

    c) 92 = _____ tens _____ units (ones)

    d) 18 = _____ ten _____ units (ones)

4 marks

6 Use the correct symbol (<, > or =) to describe these fractions.

    a) $\frac{1}{2}$ ☐ $\frac{3}{4}$ **b)** $\frac{1}{1}$ ☐ $\frac{1}{4}$

    c) $\frac{2}{4}$ ☐ $\frac{1}{2}$ **d)** $\frac{3}{4}$ ☐ $\frac{1}{4}$

4 marks

7 Solve these division number problems.

    a) 40 ÷ 5 = _____   **b)** 20 ÷ 2 = _____

    c) 10 ÷ 1 = _____   **d)** 100 ÷ 10 = _____

4 marks

8 Phillip has 26 sweets. He shares 11 sweets with his friends. How many sweets does he have left?

_____ – _____ = _____

1 mark

9 27 eggs plus 13 eggs.

_____ + _____ = _____

1 mark

10 The number is 12.

    What is $\frac{1}{4}$ of this number? _____

1 mark

11 Write the missing numbers on the stars:

65   67   70   71

3 marks

12 a) Jamil had 25 comics. He threw nine away after reading them.

How many comics did he have left? _____

1 mark

b) Jemima had 23 coins in her money box. She put six more in the box after her birthday.

How many coins are now in her money box? _____

1 mark

13 a) Count forwards in steps of 3.

| 5 | 8 | | | 17 | | 23 |

3 marks

b) Count backwards in steps of 5.

| 60 | | 50 | 45 | | 35 | 30 | |

3 marks

14 a) Double the value of 20.   _____

b) Halve the value of 20.   _____

2 marks

PS **15** On Monday Mrs Green received three letters. On Tuesday she got five letters and on Wednesday she received seven more.

How many letters did Mrs Green receive in total?

_____ + _____ + _____ = _____

1 mark

16 Use the symbols <, > or = to compare the numbers.

a) ☐

b) Twenty ☐ Twenty   c) 59 ☐ 61

17 Use the number line to solve the addition and subtraction sums.

30 31 32 33 34 35 36 37 38 39 40 41 42 43 44 45 46 47 48 49 50

a) 30 + 7 = _____   b) 34 + 12 = _____

c) 46 – 5 = _____   d) 49 – 14 = _____

18 Partition these two-digit numbers into tens and ones.

a) 11 _____   b) 98 _____

19 A piece of paper is cut into 28 equal strips.

a) How many strips would make $\frac{1}{2}$ of the piece of paper?

_____

b) How many strips would make $\frac{1}{4}$ of the piece of paper?

_____

PS **20** Martin has 10 football stickers. Jack has 10 times more stickers than Martin and Nicholas has 10 times less than Martin.

How many stickers do Jack and Nicholas have?

Jack: _____   Nicholas: _____

Marks........./54

Standard Units of Measure 1

Challenge 1

1 These hungry caterpillars are different lengths.

A

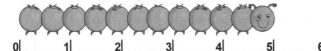

B

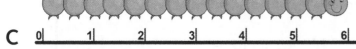

C

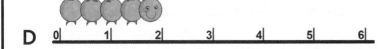

D

a) Which caterpillar is the shortest? _____

b) Which caterpillar is the longest? _____

c) Is caterpillar A longer or shorter than B? _____

3 marks

2 Join the labels to the items showing their most likely length.

about 6 m

about 10 cm

2 marks

Marks.......... /5

Standard Units of Measure 1

Challenge 2

1 Alice wants to make a fruit cake. She has measured her fruit before she makes the mixture.

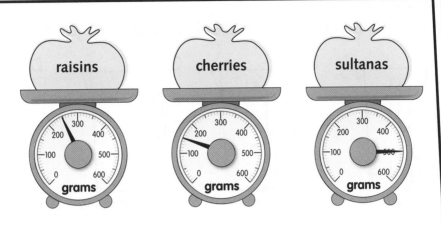

a) What is the weight of the raisins? _____ g

b) How many grams of sultanas does she have? _____ g

c) How much do the cherries weigh? _____ g

d) Which fruit has she the most of? _____

e) What is the total weight of all the fruit? _____ g

5 marks

Marks.......... /5

Challenge 3

1 Join the items to their estimated weight.

less than 2 g

about 100 g

more than 10 kg

about 3 kg

keyboard

bike

leaf

chocolate bar

4 marks

Marks.......... /4

Total marks .... /14

How am I doing?

Standard Units of Measure 2

Challenge 1

PS ⟩ **1** These jugs all contain different amounts of juice.

A

orange

B

apple

C

blackcurrant

D
lime

a) How many litres of apple juice does jug B hold? _____ l

b) If the orange juice in jug A was added to the apple juice in jug B, how much juice would there be all together?

_____ l

c) Which jug has the least amount of juice? _____

d) What would be the total capacity of all the juice?

_____ l

4 marks

Marks.......... /4

Challenge 2

PS ⟩ **1** Katie is serving cake and ice-cream. Each scoop holds 100 ml of ice-cream.

a) Alan wants just one scoop, so he would get _____ ml of ice-cream.

b) Jasmine wants 200 ml, so she would need _____ scoops.

Standard Units of Measure 2

c) Ahmed wants three scoops. That would be _____ ml of ice-cream.

d) How much ice-cream would Katie have used altogether by serving Alan, Jasmine and Ahmed?

_____ ml

e) If Katie had one litre of ice-cream to begin with, how much would remain?

_____ ml

5 marks

Marks.......... /5

Challenge 3

PS **1** If the capacity of one cup is 150 ml, what would the capacity of two cups be?

_____ ml

1 mark

PS **2** A teapot full of tea has a capacity of two litres.

How many 200 ml cups of tea could be poured? _____

1 mark

PS **3** David takes three lots of 150 ml energy drinks on his bike ride.

What is the total volume of his energy drinks? _____ ml

1 mark

PS **4** Jane needs 500 ml of ice-cream.

How many 100 ml scoops can she use? _____

1 mark

Marks.......... /4

Total marks .... /13   How am I doing?

Measurement

Measuring Time

Challenge 1

1 Join these times to the correct clock.

| half past 3 | 2 o'clock | 3 o'clock | half past 2 |

4 marks

2 What is the earliest time shown on the clocks?

_____

1 mark

PS **3** What are the intervals between the times shown on the clocks?

_____ minutes

1 mark

Marks.......... /6

Challenge 2

1 **a)** Draw the hands on these clocks to show the next three times in half hour – or 30-minute – steps.

 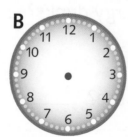  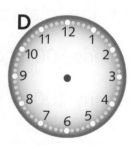

3 marks

b) How much time has passed between the first and final clock?

_____

1 mark

Marks.......... /4

44

Measuring Time

Challenge 3

1 The digital and analogue clocks need to match. They show times in the morning. Draw the hands on clocks A and B to match the digital time and write the digital time to match clocks C and D.

 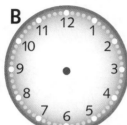  

1	2	3	4
6 : 30	7 : 00	:	:

4 marks

PS **2** It takes 30 minutes for Hannah to walk to school. How long does she spend walking to school in five days?

_____

1 mark

3 Draw the hands on these clocks to show the next three times in quarter hour – or 15-minute – steps.

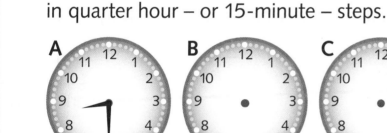 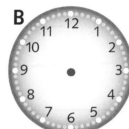 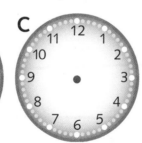 

3 marks

4 Write down these analogue times as digital times.

a) Quarter past eight. _____

b) Half past five. _____

2 marks

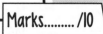 Marks........ /10

Total marks .... /20

How am I doing?

Standard Units of Money

Challenge 1

PS ⟩ **1** Jo has been saving her money for a visit to the toy shop.

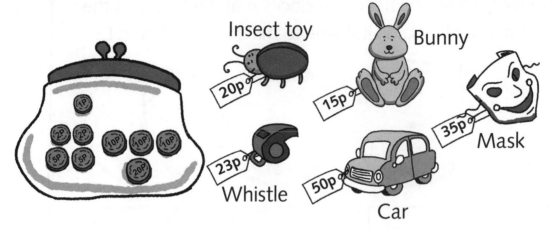

Insect toy 20p

Bunny 15p

Mask 35p

Whistle 23p

Car 50p

a) How much money does Jo have in total? _____ 1 mark

b) What can Jo buy using only one coin?

_____ 1 mark

c) The whistle costs 23p. Find two different ways to pay for it.

_____ 2 marks

d) If Jo paid for the car using five coins, which coins were they?

_____ _____ _____ _____ _____ 1 mark

Marks.......... /5

Challenge 2

PS ⟩ **1** Use the coins and items from Challenge 1.

a) Jo has the exact amount of money to buy the car and one other item. What would the other item be?

_____

b) If Jo bought the insect toy and the bunny, how much would she have left to spend?

_____

Standard Units of Money

c) How much would two insect toys cost? _____

d) Put the items in order of value from least to most.

_____

_____

4 marks

2 How much would Jo need to buy all the items?

_____

1 mark

Marks.......... /5

Challenge 3

1 These money boxes each contain different amounts.

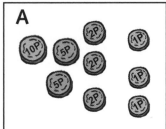
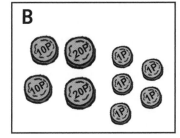
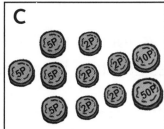

a) How much does each money box contain?
Box A: _____ p   Box B: _____ p   Box C: _____ p

3 marks

b) Ben has 50p. Find four different ways to show that amount using the coins in the boxes.

_____

_____

_____

_____

4 marks

Marks.......... /7

Total marks .... /17   How am I doing?

2-D and 3-D Shapes

Challenge 1

1 Join the shape to its name.

hexagon   triangle   pentagon   circle

4 marks

PS **2** Try to name the flat shape by its properties.

a) I have four straight sides of equal length. I am the shape of the six faces of a cube. I am a _____.

b) I have no straight sides. I have a circular edge.

I am a _____.

c) I have four straight sides and four corners. I have two short sides and two longer sides.

I am a _____.

d) I have six straight sides.

I am a _____.

e) I have three straight sides.

I am a _____.

5 marks

Marks.......... /9

Challenge 2

1 Which shape does **not** have four sides? Tick the correct answer.

A ☐   B ☐   C ☐   D ☐

1 mark

48

2-D and 3-D Shapes

2 Mark the corners on these shapes.

5 marks

Marks.......... /6

Challenge 3

1 Describe two properties of each of the flat shapes below.

a)

b)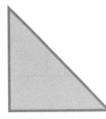

_____ _____

_____ _____

_____ _____

4 marks

2 How many faces and vertices do these solid shapes have?

A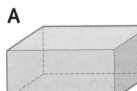

B

_____

_____

4 marks

Marks.......... /8

Total marks .... /23   How am I doing?

Different Shapes

Challenge 1

1 Complete this table. Put a tick (✓) if the property is correct and a cross (✗) if it is not correct.

Shape	Has 6 faces	Has triangular faces
Cuboid		
Pyramid		

4 marks

2 Connect the shape to its name.

sphere   cuboid   pyramid   cone   cube   cylinder

    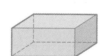

6 marks

Marks......... /10

Challenge 2

1 What shapes are these objects?

a) Clock face

b) Tin can

c) Puzzle block

_____   _____   _____

3 marks

Different Shapes

2 a) Mark the vertices you can see on this cube.

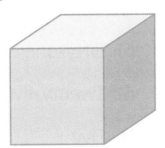

b) How many edges does a cube have in total? _____

2 marks

Marks.......... /5

Challenge 3

1 Which of these is a triangular-faced, 3-D shape? Tick the correct box.

1 mark

2 Draw two lines of symmetry on each shape.

6 marks

Marks.......... /7

Total marks .... /22   How am I doing?

51

PS Problem-solving questions

1 Write these in numerals.

    a) Sixty-three _____   **b)** Fifty-one _____

    c) Forty-eight _____   **d)** Twenty-five _____

    e) Nineteen _____   **f)** Five _____

    g) Thirty-three _____   **h)** Seventy-six _____

    i) Eighty-seven _____   **j)** Ninety _____

10 marks

2 Join these times to the correct clock.

| half past 4 | 5 o'clock | 1 o'clock | half past 7 |

A  **B**  **C**  **D**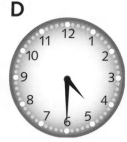

4 marks

3 Look at the rectangles.

A 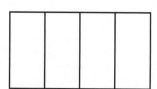 **B**  **C**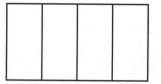

    a) Colour $\frac{3}{4}$ of rectangle A.

    b) Colour $\frac{1}{4}$ of rectangle B.

    c) Colour $\frac{1}{2}$ of rectangle C.

3 marks

4 Use the numbers 22, 12 and 34 to create addition and subtraction number sentences.

_____ + _____ = _____   _____ – _____ = _____

_____ + _____ = _____   _____ – _____ = _____

4 marks

5 Look at Connor's money.

a) How much money does Connor have in total? _____

b) Connor wants to buy some crisps. They cost 25p.
Find two different ways to pay for the crisps.

_____

_____

c) How much money does Connor have left after buying the crisps?

_____

3 marks

6 Complete the sequence of numbers by counting in tens.

a) _____ 20 _____ _____ 50 _____ 70 _____ _____ 100

b) 100 _____ 80 _____ 60 _____ 40 30 _____ _____

2 marks

7 What fraction of each cake has been eaten?

a) 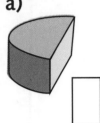 ☐

b) 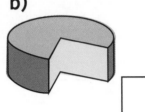 ☐

c) 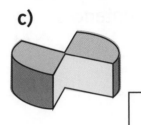 ☐

d) 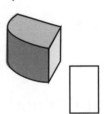 ☐

4 marks

8 Partition the two-digit numbers into tens and units (ones).

a) 83 = _____ tens _____ units (ones)

b) 29 = _____ tens _____ units (ones)

c) 16 = _____ ten _____ units (ones)

3 marks

9 How many sides, faces and corners do these shapes have?

A   B

A: Sides = _____ Corners = _____

B: Faces = _____ Corners = _____

4 marks

10 Complete these multiplications and divisions.

a) $2 \times 5 =$ _____

b) $5 \times 10 =$ _____

c) $2 \times$ _____ $= 24$

d) $10 \div 2 =$ _____

e) $20 \div 5 =$ _____

f) $20 \div$ _____ $= 10$

6 marks

11 Write in words the times shown by each clock.

a)

b)

c)  _____

d)  _____

4 marks

12 Solve this number problem. Show how you worked it out.

Andy has 16 marbles. He loses 6.

How many marbles does he now have? _____

1 mark

13 Draw a line of symmetry on this rectangle:

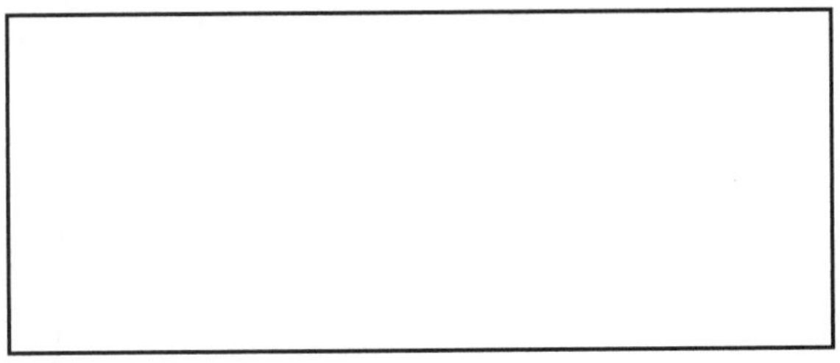

1 mark

14 Do the following calculations.

a) Add 9, 3 and 7. _____

b) Subtract 12 from 37. _____

2 marks

15 a) Draw a line to match each item to its estimated weight.

less than 20 g   melon

about 100 g   banana

more than 5 kg   strawberry

about 1 kg   sack of potatoes

4 marks

b) Which item is the heaviest? _____

1 mark

Marks........./56

55

Patterns and Sequences

Challenge 1

1 Repeat this sequence of shapes in the space below.

5 marks

2 Continue this number pattern using numbers and shading.

1	1	2	2	3	3	4	4						

3 marks

Marks.......... /8

Challenge 2

1 Look at the picture.

   a) Which number is above the

      number 2? _____

   b) Which number is to the right

      of number 2? _____

   c) Which number is below the

      number 2? _____

   d) _____ is to the left of number 2.

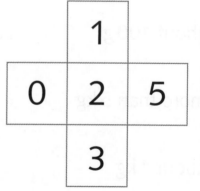

4 marks

56

Patterns and Sequences

2 a) Draw a square above the triangle.

b) Draw a circle below the triangle.

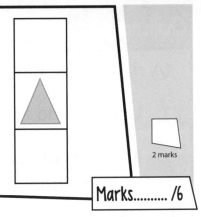

2 marks

Marks.......... /6

Challenge 3

1 Continue this sequence for the next four items.

Draw your four shapes here:

4 marks

2 Complete this grid by following the instructions.

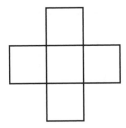

a) Place a 3 in the centre square.

b) Put a 1 above the 3.

c) Put a 5 in the square that is to the right of the 3.

d) Place a 6 below the 3.

e) Put a 7 to the left of the 3.

5 marks

Marks.......... /9

Total marks .... /23   How am I doing?

Turns

Challenge 1

(A right-angle turn is the same as a quarter-turn.)

PS ⟩ **1** Use the grid for these questions.

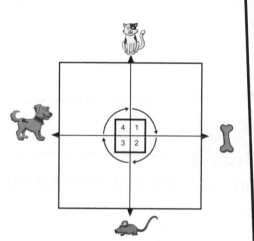

a) There are _____ right-angle turns from the cat to the mouse.

b) There are _____ clockwise, right-angle turns from the dog to the mouse.

c) The dog is _____ right-angle turns from the bone.

d) If you start at the cat and make clockwise, right-angle turns to the dog, how many do you make? _____

4 marks

Marks.......... /4

Challenge 2

PS ⟩ **1** Tim wants to ride around these race tracks.

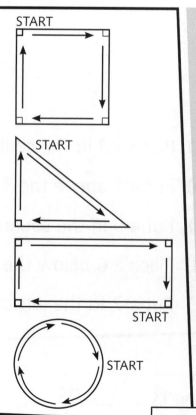

a) How many right-angle turns will Tim make on each lap of the square track?

_____

b) How many right-angle turns does the triangular track have?

_____

c) The rectangular track has _____ right-angle turns.

d) The circular track has _____ right-angle turns.

4 marks

Marks.......... /4

58

Turns

Challenge 3

1 Use the grid and follow these directions.

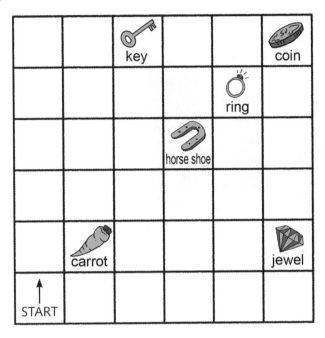

a) Beginning at the **start**, move forwards 3 squares. Make a clockwise right-angle turn and move forwards 3 squares.

You have found the _____.

b) From the **start**, move forwards 1 square. Make a right-angle turn clockwise and move forwards 5 squares.

You have discovered the _____.

c) Back at the **start**, move forwards 1 square. Make a clockwise right-angle turn and move on 5 squares. Make a right-angle, anti-clockwise turn and move forwards 4 squares.

You are now at the square containing the _____.

3 marks

Marks.........../3

Total marks .... /11

How am I doing?

Pictograms, Charts and Graphs

Challenge 1

1 This pictogram shows the favourite African animals of 12 children.

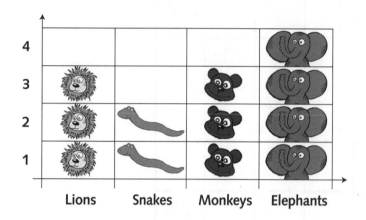

Lions   Snakes   Monkeys   Elephants

a) How many children chose the snake? _____

b) How many children chose a lion? _____

c) How many children chose a monkey? _____

d) Which animal was the most popular? _____

4 marks

Marks.......... /4

Challenge 2

1 Here is a pictogram showing votes for favourite healthy snacks.

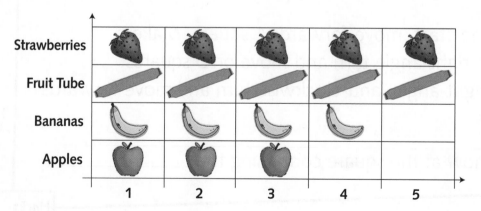

Strawberries

Fruit Tube

Bananas

Apples

     1   2   3   4   5

a) Which snack was least popular? _____

Pictograms, Charts and Graphs

b) How many votes did the least popular snack get? _____

c) How many votes were made in total? _____

3 marks

Marks.........../3

1 This block graph shows the results of a traffic survey.

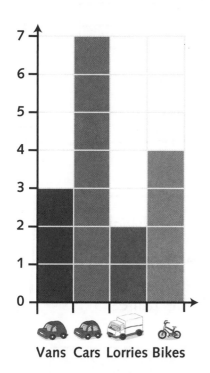

Vans Cars Lorries Bikes

a) How many vans were counted? _____

b) _____ lorries are shown.

c) How many cars are shown on the graph? _____

d) Which vehicle was seen most of all? _____

4 marks

Marks........./4

Total marks .... /11   How am I doing?

61

Gathering Information and Using Data

Challenge 1

1 A tally chart was made to show after-school activities. Use the tally to find the number of children who took part in each activity.

a) Football = _____

b) Swimming = _____

c) Gym = _____

d) Riding = _____

e) Tennis = _____

Activity	Tally	Total
Football	卌 |||	?
Swimming	卌 卌 ||	?
Gym	卌		?
Riding	|||	?
Tennis	||||	?

5 marks

Marks.......... /5

Challenge 2

1 Below is a graph that shows favourite types of sandwich.

a) Use the graph to complete the tallies in the chart.

5 marks

b) Fill in the last column to show the total of the tallies.

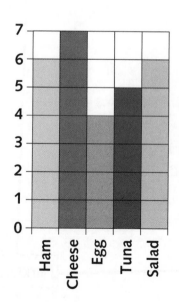

Sandwich	Tally	Total
Ham		
Cheese		
Egg		
Tuna		
Salad		

5 marks

Marks......... /10

62

Gathering Information and Using Data

1 It is Frankie's birthday and a box of food has arrived. Frankie needs to find out how much he has of each kind of snack.

key Crisps Jelly Buns Samosas Ice-cream

a) Make a tally of the food using the chart below.

Food	Tally	Total
Crisps		
Jelly		
Buns		
Samosas		
Ice-cream		

10 marks

b) Now use the data from the tally chart to make a graph showing Frankie's party food.

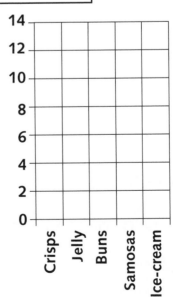

5 marks

Marks.......... /15

Total marks .... /30   How am I doing? 😊 😐 😣

1 These slippery fish are different lengths.

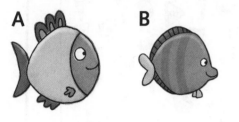
A

B   C

D

5 cm   2 cm   7 cm   3 cm

   a) Which fish is the longest? _____

   b) Which fish is the shortest? _____

   c) Is fish A longer or shorter than fish D? _____

   d) Put the fish in order from shortest to longest. _____

4 marks

2 Use the symbols <, > and = to compare the numbers.

   a) 75 ☐ 59   **b)** 14 ☐ 19

   c) 98 ☐ 98   **d)** 100 ☐ 99

4 marks

3 Find half of these numbers.

   a) Half of 10 is _____.

   b) Half of 20 is _____.

   c) Half of 16 is _____.

   d) Half of 40 is _____.

4 marks

4 Draw the next four squares in this sequence.

1 mark

5 Write the next six numbers in this number pattern.

9 9 8 8 7 7 _____

1 mark

6 Now complete this trickier number pattern.

5 5 5 5 5 4 4 4 4 _____

1 mark

PS **7** You and your friend have 12 fruit sticks.

a) Divide them up so that each of you has the same number.

How many fruit sticks would you each get? _____

b) If you shared the fruit sticks between four people, how many would each person get?

_____

c) What if three people shared the fruit sticks?

How many would each person get? _____

3 marks

8 Show how you would do question **7 a)**, **b)** and **c)** as divisions using ÷ and =.

a) _____ ÷ _____ = _____   **b)** _____ ÷ _____ = _____

c) _____ ÷ _____ = _____

3 marks

9 Colour these arrays to show the following multiplication calculations.

4 × 2 = 8

5 × 2 = 10

2 marks

65

10 Look at the circles.

 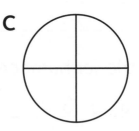 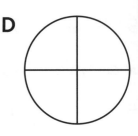

A   B   C   D

a) Colour $\frac{1}{4}$ of circle A.   **b)** Colour $\frac{3}{4}$ of circle B.

c) Colour $\frac{1}{2}$ of circle C.   **d)** Colour the whole of circle D.

4 marks

11 Count back using lots of 3 to fill in the missing numbers.

	27			18	15	

4 marks

12 You have four pairs of gloves and you get six more pairs.

How many gloves do you have? _____

I counted in steps of _____.

2 marks

PS **13** One dog has two pairs of legs.

How many pairs do five dogs have? _____

1 mark

PS **14** Complete this table. Put a tick (✓) if the property is correct and a cross (✗) if it is not correct.

Shape		Has 8 corners	Has circular faces
Cuboid			
Cylinder			

4 marks

15 a) Continue this number pattern.

33	44	55			

3 marks

b) Colour the odd numbers red and the even numbers blue.

2 marks

16 Make a tally chart of the data below. The data shows different classes and how many children drink milk.

Class 1 = 12   Class 2 = 14   Class 3 = 8   Class 4 = 10

Class	Tally	Total
1		
2		
3		
4		

4 marks

17 You are standing on the 'X' facing the snake.

	Snake	
Mouse	X	Cow
	Fox	

a) Make a right-angle, anti-clockwise turn.

You are now facing the _____.

b) Return to 'X' and face the snake. Make a clockwise half turn.

You can now see the _____.

c) Return to 'X' and face the snake. Make a three-quarter, anti-clockwise turn.

You are facing the _____.

3 marks

18 This block graph shows the different vehicles passing a school for 15 minutes.

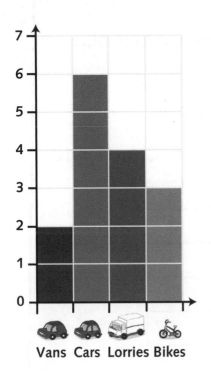

Vans Cars Lorries Bikes

a) How many bikes were seen? _____

b) How many lorries were seen? _____

c) There were _____ more cars seen than vans.

d) There were _____ more lorries seen than vans.

4 marks

Marks.........../54